BLUFFWALKER, SNAKEDOCTOR, WHISTLEPIG.

BLUFFWALKER, SNAKEDOCTOR, WHISTLEPIG.

New Poems by Jon Looney

AUGUST HOUSE/Little Rock

Books by Jon Looney:

Uphill   (1971)
Headwaters   (1979)

Some of the poems in this collection
have appeared in the *Arkansas Times Magazine*,
Equinox, *The Ozark Review*, and *Sheba Review*.

First Edition, June 1980

Cover design by D. L. Moseley
Cover photograph by Sue Hill

Library of Congress Catalog Card Number:
    80-65460

ISBN 0-935304-11-8

This book is for my Father

James Looney

8 March 1915 - 10 March 1980

1.

BLUFFWALKER, SNAKEDOCTOR, WHISTLEPIG.

In briefest form, a poem is one voice against another across a silence.
John Ciardi

My Poems

used to
dress for winter.
They are down to under-
wear now. At times, they even skin-
ny dip.
J.L.

All Day   *1.*

you have
left yourself

at dozens of
places

along the
trail:

with a spruce
two

shades
beyond green;

with a trout
(motionless) in

a clearwater
stream,

nose into
the current;

with a
waterfall sounding

like so
many

allatonce
footsteps.

(in octaves
the water falls.)

2.

dinner-time.
time

to resume
some semblance

of routine,
to bring myself

back
to myself,

in this
this extra-

ordinary world.

3.

(for all day
"I"

has been absent
— and not missed.)

(today I
have been more

than myself;
been nothing

and
everything.)

4.

From the lake
I draw water

which was
— on this

horseshoe
of mountains —

snow
(and again

will be):
I am frozen.

not from cold
but

from fear and
wonder

like the elk
which

wanders
into camp.

it is
simple

relations
which startle

(me.)

5.
opening
envelopes.

(freeze-dried
almost-food.)

dropping
their contents

into boiling
snow-water,

mixing,
I see

what recognizable
form

(like
a new day)

they assume.

6.
this has been
my day,

my
meal.

with you
whom I know

and do not
know

I share it.

For Dale Dreckman
and Debra Moseley

Bluffwalker

1.

I have been.
Missouri bluffs,

Arkansas.
(Balanced on edge

with 300 year old
cedars,

junipers
— dayold daffodils.)

All fingers, knees,
toes.

Breathless.

2.

Resting on ledge,
tented

by moss-covered
limbs.

Hands tremble.

3.

(cigarette)

4.

Thinking:
my friend

has tape
for feet

scampering
lizard-like,

effortless
as a fly

on wall.
I admit

my reluctance
before

the handhold,
the word.

Some attack
the bluff;

some embrace.

5.

Beware
the loose stone;

the branch
in the eye;

look up and
level at once.

Lightheadedness
causes

more bumps
than poison ivy.

Easy paths
deadend.

Be-aware

6.
of your breathing.

Wind on skin,
through hair

— lump in throat
muscle twitch

sunlight on lake
bird songs

wildflowers
stonesfeel

stomach-growls.
Say

hello to
your thoughts

and let them go.
For once

Be.

Mayfly

1.
day-
fly,

do you
hunger?

linger
on your way?

2.
Twenty-four
hours:

your life
span.

Born old?
Die young?

3.
Mute.
Motion

is
your song:

wing-beat
and rest,

beat
and rest,

4.
No mouth
or stomach.

You
must feed

off
of yourself,

like
a writer.

5.
But
your time

is too
short

to be
bothered

with such.
For it is

May
and Time

is
shimmering

wings.
Fly, fly, fly!

Skunk

1.
ob-beautiful-
scene

am I
which?

a house
equally divided

— but forever? —
cannot stand,

half and half
and

half against
(half.)

2.
— is no
gray.

blackandwhite
only.

blessing
one would think

to be so
clearly marked,

so obviously
certain

but,

3.
damn:
to know

no degree
no — *nth*

or shade
more

or less,
but all

ever
e-qual:

O damnable
Hell!

4.
who-
ever

of a 50:50
partnership

said
can be

no losers
(when

all lose
— equally!)

5.

better
to blow it

(off)
shoot

the moon
and lose

— or win —
once

and for good
than

foralways ever
facing

off,
double zeros

cancelling
mutually out

one
another.

6.

Aha- b.
my cousin

is
Ahab.

Snakedoctor

1.
hovers
over

water.
child-thought:

helicop
-copter.

2.
watching
makes

arms
tire.

3.
blue-bodied;
green.

eye-heads.
top heavy.

how
can they clapping-

fly
straight?

4.
wherever
you see

them,
in the reeds

or water
below

slither
snakes.

5.
they are
snakes'

friends:
fly escort;

dip
when

people
approach.

6.
got
their name

from
doctoring

hurt snakes;
slip their

claw-
tails

into wounds,
pinching them shut.

7.
sometimes
catch

couples
flyingtogether:

they
doctor

each other
too.

For Fred Pfister

Waterstrider

1.
adaptable
spider;

backwater
small pond

figure-
skater.

film-star
to the fascinated

audience-
eye.

2.
you
on a

pencil point
turn.

3.
figure
8's

among the reeds
and wood winds:

your work,
my pleasure.

4.

promenade
Gerridae

two-by-two
in country checks

and ruffles
too

swing your partner,
promenade.

5.

do you jig
in Eire,

polka
in 'Slovakia,

waltz
along the Danube,

dance to any
tune?

dan-
by without

a country.

6.

waterstrider
ripple-rider

stroke
and glide

poke
hide.

Hush!
Watcher.

hide
in the bush

till the eye
retreats.

(survival
is victory

enough.
going unnoticed,

the key.)

7.
six-legs.
(but) some

will
chide:

a spider
is

a spider
is

a
spider,

eight or
six.

8.
well-
made.

your legs
example:

hind pair
steer.

middle pair:
leg-paddles.

your actions
easy

as walking
on (h)air(s.)

9.
breathing-organs,
simple;

no need,
like some,

to wrench speech
from

breathing
tubes.

(communication
comes only

when action
fails.)

10.
a fisher of
men?

Son
of God

from you
learned,

turned
and faced

an astonished
crow -d.

For Dale Dreckman

Whistlepig

1.

groundhog
motionless.

ears
erect.

statue
of himself:

stuffed-
still.

wind
whiskers

nose.
twitch.

which
direction

danger?
man/

death
stalking,

stealing
his form,

flattening
it

peltlike
pen against page.

2.
start.
he skidders

down
an embankment

up
the other

side.
brush:hide.

comic
this chase

of imagination,
his.

high pitched
whistle

etched
cartoon-like

in cellulose
alongside

several frames,
mindfilm:

escape
retraced

in sound;
magnetic memory.

3.

poet-farmer
ridiculous,

spinning in
whirlwind

of whistlepig's
accelerations.

2.

COMINGS

Harsh, closed:
Winterearth
Is a fist.

But
Springfingers
Unfold, straighten

Into green shoots —
Jonquil, daffodil
Delicate

Crocus —
Ringgolden
Promises.

From my cold room
I open
Into this marriage.

In The Small Hours

My poems cry in the night.
How they want, hooked in my arms,
To walk the floors, soothed by
The cadence of flesh on wood.
Would they then, coaxed by rocking
And fatherly attention,
Succumb to sleep, the mild death?
Words they do not understand;
I meet their needs and they *coo*.
I take them all back to bed,
But soon their voices rise.
They know that I will follow.
My body's filled with children
Demanding their freedom.

Take-Off On Shakespeare

1.
Mid-October.
We are so hot
We have to turn on
The air conditioner
To make love.

Our long distance love
Is killing me.
We must meet more often
Than once a month.

2.
After visiting you,
I hobble around funny
For atleast a week.

I am sore.
Not at you:
From you.

It is
A tenderness I accept
With open arms.

3.
We fit together,
Lint in a navel.

Which is why when we meet
There is an eruption.
Papa called it,
"Good destruction."

And Hamlet (*aside*):
"Ah, there's the rub!"

Three In A Row

1. Tavern

You sit
playing with a
cigarette and a beer
in your hands and, in your mind: the
barmaid.

2. Colors

Her eyes
are brown; mine, green:
together we compose
the earth (soil and product.) Our son —
blue sky.

3. Sleep Teaching

Her sleep
is deep and un-
disturbed, as though no one
were in bed but her. *Careful, love,*
I learn.

Making It

If, above the music,
we could hear,
would we listen.

Our words spill on the table
like drinks and are sponged away
by courteous strangers.

I have a feeling
someone's hand is in my pocket
and the sensation is unpleasant.

Pardon me, waiter,
how long for a table?

I never come here ... it's so loud.
I can't stand the place but —

Good to see you. Whatsyournameagain?

I am patted on the back
Ole Buddy till I chip a tooth
on a glass.

Who are these dental charts
disappearing into the crowd?

No goddamn it I don't —
until I finish this one —
want another drink.

Last night I dreamed
I was smothered by a mob
of color coordinated double knit
leisure suits.

Did you — pardon — say something?
Pardon — did I?

Sleepwalking

Like submerged men we move in darkness
Weighted to an ocean's stormy floor.
Awkward as steel-helmeted divers,
Worrying over life lines and sharp
Snags, we sweat within our canvas suits.
Life, down here, carries its own light. And
Love is a rare and slippery catch.
We are tethered topside. The lines break.
And we are condemned to slowmotion
It around: bumping into opposites
We mistake for likes; loneliness we
Believe affection; beauty, beauty.
Our arms are sandbags, our eyes wrapped in
Gauze which almost stops all light. Almost.

The Coming of Sarah

After three years you leave the three S's
Of Paris ("slight frames, square shoulders, small asses")
For the Sudan sun. By steamship it is
Ten days up the White Nile to Khartoum.
You travel alone. (Your mother worrys.)
On deck at night a man sells hash. He presumes
To light your pipe and — *disappear*. Six days
Out: a young girl, her mother slaughtering
A goat, goes overboard. No trace. Drug haze:
A man a pipe with black honey filling ...
And the light of the match in the man's eye,
And the gonegirl, and the slaughtered goat share
Berth in your dreams' sweltering. They testify
(As date trees sway): 'Sarah, you are. You Are.'

Moving Men

unfold a sheet

in a curtainless and
sparsely furnished room.

— The end of a season.
Solemn as flag folding

they move
in a booted ballet

around a chair:
old and tapestry-stitched.

(Picture a great tree
protecting young

lovers in Grecian dress,
Cardea and Limentius, say,

engaged
in endless conversation.)

Beer-bellied dancers
sheetarms

outstretching
fall.

The sheet, catchingair,
billows.

A momentary firmament;
perfect, pure.

Till it collapses.

— An eggshell-thin membrane
holds us here.

— Is all
that separates.

When the corners of the sheet
settle

the room goes dark.

3.

Insomnia

Night-demon,
you drag me

from my sleep
again

and
I just want you

to know
and this

supercedes
any

loyalties mentioned
heretofore

or future
infatuations

(literary or
imagined)

and I may
change

my mind
tomorrow

but tonight

Henry Miller is
(that sweet sonofabitch)

the greatest
writer

there is
or has been

and I just may
quit my job tomorrow

thank you and
goodnight.

When I Got To Paris

I found five letters
Waiting:

Five long white fingers,
Love's hand.

But love's touch is soft,
Fleeting.

Let me see the sights,
Forget.

Ireland

The green hills roll on forever
in one great lawn.

You'd never guess
this island is a coin
or that there's a war going on.

Kruger's

Every night he drinks
At the Western-most pub
In Ireland.

Man is a creature of habit.

The Guinness is cheap,
The songs are sad, and
He knows he's closer to home.

Man is a creature of habit.

Toast

So here's to the boys
Who take their joys
And leave their troubles behind.

And here's to the boys
Who know their joys
Here in the Land of the Double-bind.

Evening Conversations

Sitting on kegs in the pub.
We put away the pints.

We talk and talk and talk
Then wait to talk again.

But it is the Guinness that speaks.
(And the open door that listens.)

Blonde Lady in the Black Dress

As the dress falls
The lady disappears.

Yellow Flag

He brings
An Iris to
His new friend. The flower
Surprises them by blooming three
Times more.

Poor Man's Fire

egg shells
turf
a bit of coal
driftwood
wads of newspaper
a cereal box
cheese wrappers
and plastic milk bottles for starters

Marie calls it "a poor man's fire"

me, I never felt so rich

The Hearth

In County Kerry, May nights
Can be cold and dark.

Two sit cross-legged on the floor.
They feed a small coal fire.

Cliffwinds tossed them together,
His lover in Connecticut
Hers in Cork.

As the darkfire smolders,
He considers the time it takes
For the black stone to be schooled
In its strength. How a longer,
Stronger earthen embrace produces a diamond.

In turn they tend the flame, carefully,
Knowing there are times a fire needs
Not fuel but space to breathe.

Screening the front of the firebox
With a section of newspaper,
She shows him how to pull more air
Beneath the coals, to catch a reluctant stone.

Two in the morning.

When the flame flickers
She sprinkles the stones with sugar.
The sweet flame dances.

"Sugar makes a fire grow,"
She explains,
"Salt puts it out."